T0146836

In *Jesus'* Arms

One Woman's Trip to Heaven

Mary E. Keenan

IN JESUS' ARMS
ONE WOMAN'S TRIP TO HEAVEN

iUniverse books may be ordered through booksellers or by contacting:

iUniverse
1663 Liberty Drive
Bloomington, IN 47403
www.iuniverse.com
1-800-Authors (1-800-288-4677)

ISBN: 978-1-5320-0112-3 (sc)
ISBN: 978-1-5320-0108-6 (e)

Library of Congress Control Number: 2016911007

Print information available on the last page.

iUniverse rev. date: 08/08/2016

To my Father in heaven
and Robert E. Detwiler,
my father in heaven.

Contents

Contents

Acknowledgments

I never entertained the fantasy of writing a book before this experience. It was through the open hearts and counsel of some very precious family and friends that I was able to make the decision to use this vehicle to share my *journey* of the summer of 2015.

My husband, Dale Keenan, quietly and nonjudgmentally listened to my account the day after my journey. He has supported and loved me unconditionally since that night, even when he has not always understood. His sacrifices to help me fulfill this mission speak to a Christlike love.

My dear friend and sister in Christ, Marguerite Davis, gave wise counsel as I sorted out the meanings of this vision, and she also provided a strong sounding board upon which to test my interpretations.

The Reverend Kevin Bowers, pastor of First Christian Church, Disciples of Christ, in Weirton, West Virginia, was always a willing listener and gave me the courage to follow through, never imposing his own viewpoints, even when I wanted them. He personifies a child of God.

My sister, Marilyn Gibble, the dedicated student of scripture whose excitement about my experience helps to buoy my spirits, was at the other end of the phone for hours, helping me process everything, and she understands me better than anyone.

Chapter 1

My Life from Conviction to Redemption

What kind of person believes she has met Jesus and taken a trip to heaven? A dying one? A holy one? A nutcase? I am certainly not holy, and I like to think I have a firm grip on reality. I am still very much alive, with the aches and pains to prove it, and I've never had a near-death experience. I don't fit the mold of church lady ... or any other mold I can think of. Those amazingly accurate Internet personality quizzes indicate that if I were an animal, I would be a cross between an otter and a German shepherd who listens to Credence Clearwater Revival. I would apparently be happiest living in Vienna if it were in the state of Hawaii and placed smack-dab in the middle of Muslim West Africa. Patrons of my art have stated that many of my paintings are inconsistent with my short "little blonde lady" appearance because the subjects are replete with images of decaying buildings and nonwhite human subjects.

What I am is a broken and flawed member of humanity who has been mended and glued back together and can now reflect on my development from thinking like a child to thinking more like an adult. Like many other people who have reached the supposed age of wisdom, I have finally developed an appreciation for how much I don't know. Everything I've done and learned was only scratching the surface of all there is to know and do. I have also learned that thinking like an adult from God's perspective has nothing to do with years lived or knowledge of the world. I've witnessed many learned adults who, having achieved much in this world, speak and act from the foundation of childish thinking. History and popular culture are replete with many famous ones.

I am a sinner. I've done some good things from the world's perspective; however, I have made choices that brought shame to myself and to my family, and I betrayed my religious upbringing. I've said and done many things I remember—and other things I don't remember—that have hurt others. I've said and done things I remember—and other things I don't remember—that have helped and uplifted others as well. I spent too many years doing things my way with the attitude that "God helps those who help themselves," doing what felt right at the time or seemed right by societal standards. I used my own head without consulting the one who had made me. I had the mind of a child well into middle age. "When I was a child, I spoke like a child, I thought like a child, I reasoned like a child" (1 Corinthians 13:11 NKJV). Fortunately, despite the fact that I have stubbornly done things my way and run myself into the mire, Christ has stubbornly remained close by to salvage me when I admitted I needed Him.

I had a tenuous relationship with the church for much of my life, struggling to remain in the fold despite feeling more comfortable to stay away much of the time. One of my first memories as a little child is of three imaginary friends—Santa, the majorette, and Jesus. I held Jesus' hand as we marched up and down the living room with the majorette, listening to John Phillip Sousa blaring from the record player. I thought the man in the robe who visited our Sunday school classroom was God. I talked to Jesus as I played, cried over stories of the crucifixion, and prayed for snow on school days.

Up until the age of fourteen or fifteen, I had an unquestioning trust in the church, attended Sunday school and catechetical class, and memorized the books of the Bible, the Lord's Prayer, the Nicene Creed, the Apostles' Creed, the Twenty-Third Psalm, and most of the liturgy. I felt safe and comfortable. I spent my Saturdays in our church office stuffing bulletins and mailers—that is, until the day an inappropriate touch from a trusted clergyman occurred. Either I failed to convey what happened to my parents, or they did not get my message—I don't remember which. What I do remember is hand-printing an anonymous scathing critique of the youth minister and placing it in the church suggestion box. During the next Sunday school class, our teacher, whom I adored, announced that someone had deposited a horrible missive in the suggestion box and that the writer was surely going to hell. I never revealed myself as the writer, because I didn't want to lose my relationship with the people in our church who meant so much to me. I remained the good girl on the surface and hid my identity as the hell-bound betrayer. I felt like a worthless imposter, and this feeling solidified at the age of sixteen after an assault by a nineteen-year-old boy at school. My parents decided not to bring any charge in order to protect me from the trials and accusations often received by victims, although I didn't understand that reasoning at the time. Since the young man suffered no consequences and was permitted to graduate with his class, the sense that I somehow caused and deserved the attack pervaded my thinking. I continued to hide the real me, the bad girl in the guise of a good one. Wrong thinking became ingrained.

As a young adult, I continued as part of the congregation in which I grew up. I continued to attend church, and I taught Sunday school. At the age of twenty, I married a boy from the same church, an older boy I started dating in the tenth grade. He was a regional football star who made me feel safe because no other fellows would bother me, not wanting to face him if they did. I felt comfortable without any pressure from the dating world while I was completing high school and he was overseas during the Vietnam War. I earned my RN license at a local Catholic teaching hospital, and then I started a career. I was doing everything right, but I felt unloved and unhappy in our marriage. I worked hard at my career, cooked dinner, kept a clean house, did the laundry and ironing, and took college courses at night. I was exhausted most of the time, and I wondered why things just were not working. I didn't know how to care for myself, and neither one of us understood what it really meant to care for each other as husband and wife. I was not mature enough to enter into marriage in the first place. I was doing the right *things*; however, I had no joy, and secretly, I knew I wasn't *worthy*.

My exhaustion and poor self-worth made the ground fertile for very bad choices. Enter a man I'll call Steven, an executive officer at my workplace. He was a much older, tall, handsome, worldly, manipulative, authoritative, and *married* Prince Charming who made me feel desirable and loved. The affair gave me an unnatural energy because of the thrill that comes with knowing you are doing something very wrong. He was highly skilled in the art of manipulation. He romanced and conquered me without much effort. I convinced myself that I could escape unhappiness by marrying this man and moving away to start a new life. Once we were married, however, that new life was just an unhappier life. Now situated in another state far away from anyone I knew, my new mate began to lose interest in an emotional or physical relationship with me, saying, "Stay out of my personal life!" I was a commodity of sorts, but that fit with my opinion of myself. We had a relationship that was a form of friendship, and I held on to it throughout our twenty-year marriage. The friendship came with betrayal, lies, emotional abuse, and threat of physical harm, abuse of pets, and isolation from my family. I chose to ignore his job losses because of the sexual harassment of other women, and I threw myself into my career, determined to make my own income and secure my own financial future. I was not going to walk out of this marriage and fail again. I couldn't appreciate the fact that continuing down a wrong path would never get me to the right place.

During the later years of our marriage, Steven grew even colder and pulled further and further away from me. Up until this point, there had been times when he seemed to want to be with me, even enjoying some vacations and having our marriage vows renewed. It would give me hope, although he still did not want an emotional or physical marital relationship. In the end, he wanted no relationship at all, refused to go for marital counseling, and told me I should get a divorce. Years before, a caring pastor counseled me to either leave the marriage or emotionally separate myself because my spouse had left our marriage in every way but the document. I didn't have the courage or emotional energy to do that, always hanging on to the times when he was kind and happy.

I finally accepted the viewpoint that I had no recourse but to file for the divorce. During the night after our property settlement, Steven died unexpectedly of an aortic aneurysm. Since he had not yet moved out of our house, I called the ambulance when he became ill and stayed with him in the emergency room of our small town hospital. There, while lying on a gurney, Steven told me that he knew he had abused me, and I now accept that statement as his apology. He was airlifted to a city hospital, and I followed by car. I could not have weathered the night of his death if not for the ministry of special friends. Two amazing women sat with me in the critical-care waiting room, telling ridiculous and sometimes risqué jokes to make me laugh in the midst of rather horrid circumstances. After the hospital staff announced that Steven had stabilized for the time being, one of the women took me to her home near the hospital and tucked me into her guest bed for the night, lying beneath a crucifix. That symbol reminded me of Jesus' amazing love and brought a moment of peace that allowed sleep to come. When we were awakened in the middle of the night with *the call*, my friend drove me to the hospital while I screamed, stayed with me while I spent some time with the body, and then drove me to my home, which was about twenty-five miles away. Later that morning other friends brought my car home and stayed until my sister, Marilyn, arrived from out of state. The Lord was faithful in this time of extreme need, and He used those friends to carry me through that experience.

There was, however, no time or allowance for bereavement. I felt relief from Steven's presence but guilt for feeling the relief. My family came and went, thinking perhaps that since we were divorcing, my recovery from his death would not be difficult. I plunged back into work and became very busy. Though I had needed relief from Steven's presence, that didn't mean I had not loved and cared about him. Everything around me went on as before, everything but me.

Through prayer, my personal relationship with God had grown stronger as the marital relationship had grown weaker. I found comfort in my faith through those years, but I never fully allowed myself to accept God's forgiveness. During those years, I returned to school to earn my baccalaureate and master's degrees, directed the organization of one of the first hospice programs in the United States, and became a licensed nursing home administrator. I held managerial and consultative positions in corporate health care, managed a dual-diagnosis psychiatric unit, taught as an associate university professor, and engaged in other endeavors to further my experience and knowledge. Despite these efforts, none made me feel truly worthy. Holding on to these feelings of worthlessness had grown into a pernicious arrogance, so that I embraced the sense that I was beyond God's promises of redemption.

I am not going to reiterate all the hurtful details of those twenty years because to recount it all would serve no useful purpose to you or me. In recent years, I confronted the hurt with the help of a Christian counselor. I still have occasional nightmares relating to my former life, and I must guard against seeing the present through eyes of the past. The wounds have healed, but their evidence remains. That's okay because I know the scars are only part of this old life. They will disappear for the next life. They are also a reminder of how much I've matured from the person I once was.

In the months after Steven's death, I was numb to my own feelings and the feelings of other people. Shortly before he died, I sought out a minister to help me with the verbal and emotional abuse I was experiencing. He opened his home to me, and I spent time with his family when I couldn't face being in my own home. After his death, I learned Steven had told our friends in the community that I was cheating on him and divorcing him for another man. This lie spread like a virus. It was the worst betrayal, worse than his infidelities. I had vowed I would never do that to another man. I could forgive Steven but not myself. The minister who had once opened his home to me shut me out, saying, "How can you live with yourself?" What people thought about me was so important to my self-esteem, and my reputation was once again ruined! I felt unworthy of anyone's caring, and I denied my need to grieve or heal from years of hurt. Instead of fully turning to God, I turned to alcohol and a series of shallow relationships with several men. I had good times with my friends and floated on a sort of high. One friend said, "Mary, I think your social life is interfering with your professional life." Another said, "I think you get most of your calories in liquid form." I laughed off the comments, thinking I was in full control. Deep down, I was empty.

During a snowy, cold New Year's Eve prayer vigil, I knelt before our church's altar and prayed for someone to love me unconditionally, someone who would accept all of my flaws and cherish me despite my brokenness. That person was God Himself, but He had to show this to me through another person in order for me to believe it. After a weekend of so-called partying, feeling empty and tired, I received a phone call from the young mechanic who had worked on my car the previous day. I thought, "Oh no, what's wrong with my Jeep that the garage forgot to tell me?" The Jeep was fine. He was asking me for a date. I was at my lowest point. I felt used, and I was finished with any relationship with a man. He didn't fit my criteria of dateable men either. He was a blue-collar joe, very *country*, younger, and far from wealthy. Something, however, told me that this was different and that I should follow that instinct. I reluctantly agreed to meet him at a restaurant in a nearby city. However, I refused to ride in his vehicle. I wanted to know I could get away if needed. We entered the parking lot at the same time, and he approached my Jeep to open the door for me. As I looked at Dale, a quiet voice distinctly said, "This is the person you asked me for." Here was a quiet, humble man, small in stature, with a tender voice and guileless eyes. In the restaurant we kept ordering more food because we didn't want to stop talking. Before that meal, I had little appetite for well over a year. Food tasted good again! I felt no *teenage* romantic infatuation. My feet weren't in the clouds, and there was no spellbound euphoria, just a secure, peaceful knowledge that if I was obedient, I would know love. We have just celebrated our twentieth anniversary.

This marriage, arranged by God, has taught me the meaning of Christ's love. My husband loves me as Christ loves the church. My healing kicked into high gear the day we met, and it continues today. God has gradually presented the issues I needed to address that separate me from Him, and He is helping me resolve them with His guidance. This includes forgiving the people who, because of their own brokenness, contributed to my brokenness. God has turned the potential obstacles in this marital relationship with Dale, such as family issues, my debilitating back injury, and intrusive bad memories, into home improvement projects that strengthen our marriage and my relationship with Him. I now understand that the unconditional love and feelings of fulfillment I so craved were always there in Christ. He has always been there and never given up on me. He also taught me that I had to fully trust in Him before He could truly dwell in me and me in Him. I am not unique. The same love is there for all of us if we not only hear but also trust Christ's words of salvation. I do not need a husband and marriage to be a whole person, but this marriage was part of God's method to bring me to wholeness. I can now be happy wherever I am. My needs are met, and my wants barely make the priority list. The fact that we must so often lose ourselves in order to find ourselves is so true. The *self* is so much freer, more powerful, more self-aware, more joyful, and more creative when connected to its creator! I was a stubborn case for the Lord, but fortunately, He didn't hold it against me. There is no one who can't also share in the same power, freedom, insight, joy, and creativity!

Life is so difficult when we try to navigate it on our own or when we try to use a map made by someone other than God. Life's navigator is our choice.

I have been compelled to ask, "Why me, Lord? Why have you chosen me to share this message? There are certainly better, more capable people who can do this, people with greater faith, greater commitment, greater physical endurance, better writing and verbal communication skills. Life was so much easier before." I've felt like Jonah, wanting to run away and hide, but doing so leaves me sleepless. The more I resist God about this, the more I become aware of my arrogance in questioning God's message and directive. Thinking back to the biblical prophets to whom He gave visons, God chose flawed people who sinned as greatly as they loved the Lord. The only thing I do know is that I talk to God all the time. I give Him my thoughts, and I converse with Him throughout the day as though He is in the room with me. Reflecting back, it is like the imaginary friend Jesus I had as a child, but the relationship has now matured. I don't have a special time of day to sit, meditate, and pray. Maybe I should. It's an ongoing conversation filled with the petty things of the day, my deepest secrets, my rants and anger, my pleas for help, for others' healing, for family, and for the world, and proclamations of how much I love Him when I look at the sky and the beauty around me. I am beginning to learn to listen for what He says to me and to avoid cluttering the conversation with my own noise. Like the country song, He likes hearing about me, me, me. But occasionally, He wants to talk about Him! Fortunately, there is an eternity ahead in which to revel and develop a relationship more fulfilling than any other could ever be.

The Lord has given me so much. We are told in Luke 12:48 (NIV), "From everyone who has been given much, much will be demanded; and from the one who has been entrusted with much, much more will be asked." In the second week of July 2015, my Savior showed me that He trusted me enough as His child to give me a responsibility that I cannot ignore. That responsibility is to share some of the many things He showed and entrusted me with on a summer night, to remind us that the messages He gave us more than two thousand years ago through scripture are true and relevant today more than ever. I am not a biblical scholar, and that may be part of the reason He chose me to take this trip. I didn't have the detailed scriptural knowledge to construct such an experience in my mind. I didn't have a dream that represented my interpretations of scripture, but instead I had an experience that required I research scripture to understand.

"God has always shown us that these messages are true by signs and wonders and various miracles and by giving certain special abilities from the Holy Spirit to those who believe; yes, God has assigned such gifts to each of us" (Hebrews 2:4 NIV).

Chapter 2

Carried in Jesus' Arms

On July 4, 2015, my husband, Dale, and I went to the lakes region of Ontario, Canada, for a fishing trip. The lake we visited was the same lake to which my father had taken our family every year when he was alive. Dad died in 1976. Dale never had the opportunity to meet him. Both men were avid fishermen, so I felt good about Dale experiencing the essence of my father, fishing in the same lake Dad so dearly loved. Upon arrival, we quickly unpacked the car, and then we headed out to our rental boat to get in some fishing before nightfall. Let me give you some backstory. When I was about eleven years old, I caught a giant bass that made Dad and me quite excited. It was late when we returned to the dock, and since we didn't have adequate refrigeration in the log cabin, Dad decided to leave the fish swimming on a stringer so it would remain fresh until we could clean it in the morning. I ran to the dock upon awakening the next morning and pulled up the chain to find nothing but a white skeleton. I cried, but I think Dad was even more disappointed. He blamed himself for years after that.

Dale only took the boat out into our resort's small section of the lake, and not far from the dock because he didn't trust the sputtering motor. Out of a chivalrous mind-set, he baited my hook. I cast the line and instantly had a huge strike. With a surprising fight on my hands, I reeled in a giant bass. My first thought was, *Dad knows we're here.* This was not the end of the experience, however. Each time either Dale or I cast our lines, a large fish literally jumped onto the hook, and we released each one. We ran out of the bait Dale had purchased to last a few days. Our wrists and arms were tired from reeling. We returned to the dock after less than an hour. Upon return to shore, we told our story to two young fishermen from the neighboring cabin. They immediately took their boat to the same location on the lake to try their luck, but they returned and said they caught nothing but a few small sunfish and perch. A small voice said, "I will make you a fisher of men." I wondered why that thought appeared in my head and concluded it was just a thought.

The Giant Bass

The night of July 7, after an evening of *normal* but good fishing, we turned in to bed at around ten o'clock, and I drifted off to sleep after reading my e-book. I do not know at what time the vision or journey began. When the experience ended, I was wide awake, and I felt compelled to write down what I'd seen and heard before I forgot something important. I arose and quietly walked in the dark to the tiny cabin's kitchen area so as not to wake Dale. I turned on no lights as I rummaged for a tablet and pen. I sat down to write at the kitchen table. There was a night-light over the sink area that enabled me to see where I was placing the pen on paper, but there was insufficient illumination to see the letters. As I began to write, it seemed as though the pen took control. My hand could barely keep up with the pen. It was as though it knew in advance what I was about to put down. After several pages of this frenetic writing, I placed the tablet in my bedside drawer and went to sleep. In the morning I retrieved the writing, thinking that it was doubtful that any of it would be decipherable. The words appeared loose and messy, but to my amazement, they were fully legible.

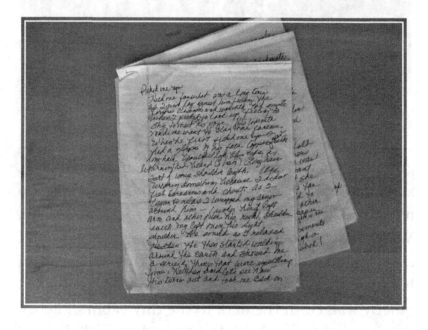

The day after this *journey*, my body felt as though I had completed a ten-mile hike over rough terrain. Dale kept asking me if I was all right because my face had a strange look. "You look funny," he said. "Like a deer in the headlights." I felt struck and shaken. I waited until later in the day to tell him about the previous night. I first needed to spend some time processing what had occurred. I felt drained, and I slept for several hours that afternoon. It felt as though I had been up all night. I suppose I was. For days thereafter, I had a distinct feeling of not being a part of the world, wondering exactly how I was supposed to go about being here after having been there and how I was supposed to proceed with the task I'd been charged to carry out.

I also asked, "Why me?" As mentioned in the last chapter, I'm not what you'd classify as a devout church lady who regularly and consistently goes to women's meetings, serves on committees, attends weekly Bible study, goes to choir practice every Wednesday night, and sings in the choir every Sunday. In fact, while I was once helping a friend get ready for a churchwomen's meeting at her home, she actually stated, "I'm not even going to pressure you into staying and participating in this because I know you wouldn't like it." The attendees were all supposed to wear their favorite aprons and share stories about each. Not my bailiwick!

I replied to her, "Thank you so much. When you decide to serve Coors Light instead of pink punch and cookies, maybe I'll be there." She laughed and lovingly sent me on my way. I'm more comfortable spending available time helping out at the Salvation Army. Do not get me wrong. Those church ladies were wonderful people who enrich Christ's church and showed me love and acceptance. I'm thankful for them and their service. It is just a matter of my comfort level and finite energy reserves. So again, *why me?*

Jesus did say that He desires mercy and not sacrifice and that He did not come to call the righteous but sinners to repentance (Matthew 9:13 NKJV). How will I continue with this mission? Where will Christ lead me as I try to carry out His purpose in this? I must maintain trust that He will show me each step of the way as I take it despite the fact that I would prefer a detailed guidebook of each step, twist, and turn in the process.

I've recounted the experience in this chapter without interjecting the thoughts I've had since thinking, praying, and studying its messages. I've neither included clarifications nor expanded on some of the descriptions of people and places, thinking that it was important to retain as closely as possible the original text as written the night of my *trip*. I did this so you can more easily consider what it means to you without the distraction of my viewpoints. In subsequent chapters I will provide a more detailed description of what I saw and discuss some of my personal understandings that came out of further reflection, study, and prayer.

The Vision

I saw a tall man who was at least two feet taller than me, dressed in a white robe. His face was rounded with full cheeks and high cheekbones, with shoulder length wavy reddish-brown (light copper) hair parted in the center, short beard, light brown skin, and blue eyes.

He picked me up and held me in His arms. I [was] on my back with head against His left upper chest and knees draped over His right arm. I felt like I was the size of a small child. He stood still and held me for a while as I just lay against Him. I was at first tense and uneasy while trying to understand what just happened. As I lay against Him, I began to feel a glorious closeness and warmth. I peeked up to look at His face. He looked down at me with a small loving smile, but I quickly buried my head into His chest, feeling too shy to meet His gaze. The blissful feeling I experienced made me want to stay there forever. I did not feel His skin, only the robe against which He held me. I realized this was Jesus.

As I began to relax, I wrapped my arms around Him, with my right arm under His left arm, and my left arm over His right shoulder. He smiled at me as I relaxed and gained the confidence to look at His face. He then started moving across the earth and showed me a series of horrible vignettes that were extremely upsetting to me. I don't think I could have tolerated them had I not been in His arms. He then said, "Let's see how these things turn out," and returned with me to each episode to discover that each one had been turned to a positive and happy resolution. I do not want to remember any specifics of what I saw. Nor do I think I am supposed to.

As we moved across the earth, He showed me people working in their daily lives. The only one I clearly remember was a woman who appeared to be a fortune-teller. Jesus proclaimed in a jolly manner, "Here's My bad one and My good one." He introduced me to the lady fortune-teller who was holding a card. She told me she was the bad one. On the card there was a little laughing lady who appeared to be having the greatest fun. Jesus introduced her to me as an angel. Jesus told her to tell me what her assignment was. She laughingly told me that her assignment was the fortune-teller. She also jokingly stated that she was "like an indentured servant," laughing as if her statement were something of a joke, and Jesus laughed with her. He then asked her to share some of her previous assignments with me. She held up a long, narrow sheet of paper with many names listed down its length. Jesus continued joking and laughing with the angel as we moved away.

We then started rising, and as we ascended, I became aware of what seemed like a sphere over my head with three oval (on the horizontal) windows—one directly in front, one to my left, and another to my right. When I attempted to look out the front window, a small hand appeared outside the window to block my view. The same then happened for the left and right windows. We stopped rising at a place Jesus told me contained both joy and sadness.

I saw a line of confused-looking people in blue clothing walking in a line under guard. The guards were large imposing men, but they were not carrying weapons that I could see. The people who filed past me appeared to be East Asian, with one woman wearing the traditional straw hat seen on field workers. No one told me, but I had the impression that this was not a permanent place for anyone there, that this was a place for learning. Here there was also a flurry of confusingly rapid activity with many people milling around.

A small group of us was then gathered and ushered through a door into a quiet place where we met a seated panel, including some of the people I had seen on my earthly round with Jesus. A leader introduced the other panel members, including a tall, handsome, very dark-skinned man named Mask. While being introduced, Mask's beautiful face morphed into a rustic, brown, flat African tribal mask with slits for eyes. Mask explained that the handsome face was only for his earthly work and that he had chosen to have the cracked, brown, distorted face where we were to remind him of the things he once did and the way he had once been.

I was then rapidly moved, giving me a feeling of being sucked or *whooshed* to another place. The sensation was almost dizzying. Here I observed many people involved in all types of activities in rapid succession. At times I found myself walking with another person, a female. I found I bounced when I stepped and had a bit of trouble controlling my trajectory. It was so easy to bounce up stairs. My companion laughingly told me, "It takes a little getting used to." As we spent time in that area, things were conveyed to me little by little, like a mental puzzle. I was told, "Be moderate," more than once. I was also told a Bible verse about sharing what had been revealed to me ... and again to be moderate.

I and the other members of my group who previously met with the panel were once again before them. The person who previously introduced Mask asked us one by one if we figured out our assignments. I was so caught up in discerning what my own answer was to be that I didn't pay close attention to the others' answers. I remember the individual beside me saying something to the effect that he was to bring happiness to other people. I was thrilled and anxious to share what I had learned. The blissful feeling of being in Jesus' arms was still present. I answered that I was to share this experience with the world. The panel then reiterated, "Be moderate."

After learning our assignments, we found ourselves walking along a great corridor in the midst of a multitude of other people. We walked up to a series of two vertically rectangular portals, through which I could only see light. As I approached the first set of portals, I heard a man somewhere behind me in the crowd state that it was important to select the correct door. Not able to discern a difference between the two portals and feeling anxiety about this, I closed my eyes and allowed myself to remember the blissful sensation of being in Christ's arms and found myself whooshed through a portal. Continuing on to the next set of portals or gates, I suddenly found that a man was trying to pull me into a portal by my right hand. A good-looking but malevolent being was pulling the man's right hand, while the man's left hand pulled mine. I yanked my hand out of his and stepped back to watch. Jesus was standing to my right, and the man was to my left. The man was looking at Jesus with a questioning expression. Jesus said to him, "It's your choice," and the man allowed himself to be pulled into the portal by the malevolent being. I again closed my eyes, remembering being held in Christ's arms, and was whooshed through the next portal ... and then another.

While on this transit through the portals, I recognized that a person who was part of our group and also had an assignment was someone I was acquainted with on earth, someone I knew but never had a desire to get to know. I attempted to make contact with her during our transit but was unsuccessful. I didn't see her again. Upon return to the earthly dimension, I ran into people I had met as workers in the other realm, one being a beautician.

I awoke to a dark night, fully alert and feeling fully charged and compelled to get up. (During the journey upward in the sphere with Jesus, my husband called my name and asked if I was all right. I opened my eyes and was in bed with him. After reassuring him, I closed my eyes and immediately felt the whooshing sensation and was back to exactly where I was before. The "earthly dimension" referenced in the last paragraph was the same dimension I had experienced while being carried over the earth by Jesus. I haven't recognized people from the journey in my regular everyday life.)

"Blessed are those who have not seen and yet have believed" (John 20:29 NKJV).

Chapter 3

Are Visions from God?

It is my hope that when you read my reflections and understandings about this vision, you will use them as impetus for your own renewed spiritual journey by talking with God (listening and praying) and studying scripture. I believe that there are many layers of meaning to this journey experience and that it creates questions not answered here and can spur topics of discussion. I hope it will help bring you into a closer relationship with Christ. If you are committed to dogma that is unique to a particular church, you may find some of my comments objectionable. Explore your reaction to my words. Use your reactions to delve further into scripture and to explore and discuss your relationship with Christ. Strive to look at scripture, including the Old Testament, through the perspective of Christ and His life while He was in our dimension. I believe having a relationship with Him is the most intimate we can experience. Belief in Christ takes precedence over any other doctrinal differences we may have—belief that Jesus is the living Son of the living God, that He wants a personal relationship with each of us, and that He came to give those of us who believe in Him eternal life.

What I refer to as a vision is a visual message. It may or may not include an auditory message. It may be one picture, a moving picture with sound, or an interactive experience involving many senses. People have experienced visions from God throughout history. The paramount issue has been listeners' responses to the messages of those visions, discernment about whether the visions came from God, from the Deceiver, or from some sort of brain dysfunction. Although it would be extremely presumptuous to compare myself to the great prophets, their examples help me find the courage to share my visions with you. The kings and intellectuals of their time accused our venerated prophets of being possessed by demons or speaking for Satan just as Jesus was. As a believer much lesser than them, I can certainly expect nothing less.

I think that the test of discernment here is to look at the fruits of the vision experience. Does the vision bring its recipient to greater faith in God? Does the vision have resonance for other believers? Does scripture support the vision's message? Does the vision engender a deeper understanding of scripture? Is the experience really a vision? I think that a true vision is clear to the recipient, devoid of muddled dreamlike qualities with messages that conflict with one another. For example, in dreams, I may find myself acting out variations of the same situation over and over again as I subconsciously work out a problem or life issue. A vision for me is the opposite of that. It is specific and sharply focused, vivid in detail, to the point and startling. At its end, I open my eyes, fully alert, feeling compelled to get up out of bed. (Read the book of Ezekiel to see multiple examples of the specificity of visions that come from the Spirit.)

All the visions I have experienced brought me to clearer understanding of God's written Word and also strengthened my relationship with the Lord. It is my belief that all my visions came from the Counselor, the Spirit, whom I also refer to as Comforter. "But the Counselor, the Holy Spirit whom the father will send in my name, will teach you all things and will remind you of everything I have said to you" (John 14:26 NIV). The journey that started out in Jesus' arms, however, was a unique encounter with the person of Christ as well as the Holy Spirit. I could see, touch, and feel Him. I felt physical as well as spiritual comfort and strength. I had no interest in looking anywhere but up at his face from the perspective of a child who was being carried, a face that carried all the subtleties of human expression. There was no dreamlike quality to Jesus, the living man.

For the remainder of this book, I will discuss my thoughts based upon study and reflection on this experience as well as contextual scriptural references that have meaning to me. The admonitions during the journey to "be moderate" preclude me from explicitly writing down all the meanings, impressions, and scriptural references I've personally drawn from this vision and previous vision messages. I anticipate and hope that you will come away with your own thoughts or reminders of other scripture passages as you read. It is my hope that others' perspectives of my vision experiences will help me broaden my own understanding and faith as well as yours.

"The man without the Spirit does not accept the things that come from the Spirit of God, for they are foolishness to him, and he cannot understand them because they are spiritually discerned" (1 Corinthians 2:14 NIV).

[Please note that the subsequent chapters and sections will be introduced by corresponding quotations from the writing done on the night of the vision.]

Chapter 4

We Are Little Children

"I saw a tall man who was at least two feet taller than me, dressed in a white robe. His face was rounded with full cheeks and high cheekbones, with long wavy reddish-brown (light copper) color hair parted in the center, beard, light brown skin, and clear blue eyes."

He was gigantic and powerful. I liken it to being a small child looking up at a large professional football player. His was not the aesthetic image we usually see depicted on the cross, not even the slender image we often see of the Good Shepherd. He was a great, powerful, muscular man whose physique more approximated Dwayne "The Rock" Johnson. Although I am an artist who does portraiture, I was not instructed to paint Christ's likeness and therefore will not do so. I think that if I focused on His appearance, I would be distracted from focusing on His message. I may have adored the image. I think it is significant, however, to consider that Christ is strong, big, and powerful.

I've read different descriptions of what Jesus looked like to other people who have experienced visions of heaven, and they are different from mine. That we each recognized someone we knew to be Jesus is of most importance since *who* He is bears more importance than what He looks like in our visions. When Jesus appears at the end of the ages, we will see our magnificent King in all His glory, and there will be no speculation as to His appearance.

"He picked me up and held me in His arms. I [was] on my back with head against his left upper chest and knees draped over his right arm. I felt like I was the size of a small child. He stood still and held me for a while as I just lay against Him. I was at first tense and uneasy while trying to understand what just happened. As I lay against Him, I began to feel a glorious closeness and warmth. I peeked up to look at his face, he looked down at me with a small loving smile, but I quickly buried my head into his chest, feeling too shy to meet his gaze. The blissful feeling I experienced made me want to stay there

forever. I did not feel his skin, only the robe against which he held me. I realized this was Jesus."

When I looked up at His face, His smile was the quiet, closemouthed smile you see on the faces of parents or grandparents when they're holding their babies or new grandchildren. He emanated a strength and assurance that made me feel entirely safe. When I feel the need for comfort, I now just close my eyes and imagine I am back in His arms. Picture the small boy who is at a public event like a county fair with his father. He is filled with wonder at everything he sees and is eager to get away from Dad's control and try every new thing until he's confronted with a scary-looking stranger, loud and unfamiliar noises, or so much activity that he cannot comprehend it all. The child runs to Daddy, buries his face in Dad's legs, and begs Dad to pick him up. That is how I now feel about Jesus when life starts to get a little too crazy. It would be easy to just rest in that feeling and do nothing, but I must keep sight of my purpose and move ahead with this mission despite the fact that I do not fully understand where this is leading me.

I am reminded of the familiar image of Christ holding the lamb in His arms, representing us. Jesus' words in John 10:11–18 (NKJV) are so powerful. In them, He refers to Himself as the Good Shepherd who knows His sheep and loves them so much that He would sacrifice His own life to protect them. Not only would He protect His own flock, but He would also offer the same protection to other sheep outside the fold by bringing in those who hear His voice and come to His call. How does Christ want us to become like little children? I think part of the answer lies in focusing on Him, acting and believing based upon our relationship with Him, and mimicking Him because we love and trust Him. Is this not how a child really learns to live, by modeling him or herself after a parental role model? When we ignore a positive parental role model and try to act on our own understanding, we end up needing more and more stringent laws and rules of behavior, which are never as effective as having a people who are internally motivated to respect, honor, serve, and love one another. It is a difference between religion and faith. Religion is rooted in law. Faith is rooted in belief.

Religion is a system of study and practice that forms a platform whereby people can worship together, practice, express, and share their beliefs. Our Christian religion provides a framework of values and mores upon which we can order our lives, upon which we have built a society that can freely worship God, and in which we are free to openly pursue a relationship with the Creator and nurture others toward a relationship with Christ. We run into trouble when religious practice is mistaken for faith, when we mistake the sheep pen for the shepherd. For example, it may be part of the mission of a Christian church to help feed the needy. Do I donate food to my church's food bank because I am supposed to in order to be an upstanding member of my church and to demonstrate my Christianity? On the other hand, do I help stock the food bank even when no one is looking because Christ lives within me and I feel compelled to do what He would do? Does the church provide a vehicle whereby I can express my faith? When I go to worship, do I place praise of Him above pride in my own or my church's accomplishments or contributions? Do I mistakenly think attendance at weekly church services or attending church meetings guarantee me a place in heaven?

How does the church family behave as little children, as the sheep in His pasture? Is the church my social club where I can be with like-minded people of similar status and receive reinforcement for my opinions and lifestyle? Does it make rules or engage in unspoken group exclusivity about the kinds of people it accepts, involving dress, education, politics, and wealth? Or is the church my family of brothers and sisters with whom I just may have few things in common other than the fact that we belong to the same family, recognize Father God is in charge, and want to please Him? As small children, we may squabble but still play together. Like little children, we accept anyone who wants to play with us, having a blind eye to race, ethnicity, or social status. We come together and do what Dad says because we accept His authority over all others. We support each other in trials such as physical and mental illness, divorce, bankruptcy, death, etc. We are also joyful at the good fortune of one another, and we do not marginalize those we may perceive as more gifted, wealthy, or successful than ourselves.

This does not mean we approve of sin in one another, but we accept each other regardless of the place one may be on the path to becoming more like Christ, our role model. This is because we are all short of that goal on our own paths. Recognizing the presence of sinfulness, we do not close the door to the church family's home on a sinner. We do not have to agree with everything our brothers and sisters do, and it is okay to voice our disagreement from a position of love. But we continue to love them and do not throw them out of the family, and we certainly do not proclaim that they are condemned to hell. One who may disrupt worship, drive wedges between members, and otherwise act against the body of Christ has separated him or herself from the family and may be asked to leave until a time when he or she wants be part of the body of Christ. These people should be dealt with individually and counseled one-on-one. When they turn their backs on the family and throw themselves out, we must make sure they know there are seats at the table for them when they decide to come back.

You may say, "Our church's doors are always open to welcome any who want to worship with us. We certainly are not a social club!" Your building's doors are open to anyone, but are your people open to everyone who wants a relationship with Christ? When you have a church dinner, do your members sit with their extended birth families and longtime friends who have gone to your church for generations while ignoring the couple they don't know very well? Do longtime members go ahead and do the work of the church without showing newer members how to help and then complain that they have to do it all while others go to worship and do nothing else? Do some longtimers feel certain functions belong to them? Do they have trouble finding something for newer parishioners to do because they are so accustomed to working among themselves? On the other hand, when a newer member takes up a task, is he or she overwhelmed with requests to do more and more? To avoid the guilt of not doing enough, does that person stop contributing his or her time or stop attending worship altogether? Do longtime members plan church projects among themselves before a meeting because it is easier to work with people they know and then discount or give lip service to the suggestions or viewpoints of newer members at the formal meeting? Do you find prospective or newer members sitting by themselves before worship while the longtimers are making the rounds and happily chatting with one another? The church's doors are not on its building. They are on the hearts of its parishioners.

If you do not have a church family, please keep looking for a church where you feel welcome. Please do not give up by saying there is no point in going to church because churches are full of hypocrites and sinners. We are all hypocrites and sinners! We need one another. When something happens at church that makes you feel uncomfortable or unwanted, speak up and say how you feel about it. If you cannot work it out and still feel unwelcome, leave, but look for another church family. We cannot make it through the coming years apart from God's family any more than a two-year-old could successfully survive apart from a supportive family. I've fallen short in being the kind of welcoming older member I should have been, and I have more frequently been the newer member who has sat in someone else's seat or showed up to help only to find my presence more of a complication than a blessing. These situations are the result of people's shortcomings, not God's, so don't throw out the baby with the proverbial bathwater.

"He called a little child and had him stand among them. And he said: 'I tell you the truth, unless you change and become like little children, you will never enter the kingdom of heaven. Therefore, whoever humbles himself like a child is the greatest in the kingdom of heaven'" (Matthew 18:34 NIV).

Chapter 5

All Will Be
Okay in the End

"As I began to relax, I wrapped my arms around Him, with my right arm under His left arm and my left arm over His right shoulder. He smiled at me as I relaxed and gained the confidence to look at His face. He then started moving across the earth and showed me a series of horrible vignettes that were extremely upsetting to me. I don't think I could have tolerated them had I not been in His arms. He then said, "Let's see how these things turn out," and returned with me to the place of each episode to discover that each one had been turned to a positive and happy resolution. I do not remember any specifics of what I saw. Nor do I think I am supposed to."

This reminds me of the passage "The eternal God is your refuge, and underneath are the everlasting arms. He will drive out your enemy before you, saying 'Destroy him'" (Deuteronomy 33:27 NIV). It's not difficult to list the horrors occurring in our communities and across the world. Sitting in front of the TV and listening to news feeds could throw anyone into depression, anger, and fatalism. The impact of terrorism and mass shootings, natural disasters, the scourge of drug addiction, the oppression of extreme poverty and hunger, materialism, extreme busyness, fears about climate change, and so on—thinking on all these things and their sequelae can cause us to lose hope. We can identify signs of the end of ages and find ourselves gripped with fear. But then we can revisit those fears and look at them for the birth pains that they are—Satan and his minions grabbing all they can to cheat God out of His children while they can before Christ ushers in a new world.

How do we keep from faltering and giving way to fear? How do we fight the Enemy? Turn to Ephesians 6:10–13. We are told to put on God's armor, which is the belt of truth, the breastplate of righteousness, the shield of faith, and the helmet of salvation and to take up the sword of His Word. We cannot fight the Enemy by ourselves without God. "I can do all things through him who strengthens me" (Philippians 4:13 NRSV). We cannot reason with, argue with, or compromise with evil. With Christ's help, we can place ourselves in His arms, remain obedient to His Word and voice, uphold fellow Christians regardless of denomination, refuse to be confused by false doctrine, and turn to prayer and scripture for guidance. When we fight against evil, we can be confident in our leader. By placing complete trust in Christ's plan for our salvation, no one can take our faith away, no matter what is done to the current physical world and us. Remember Paul's words: "And we know that in all things God works for the good of those who love him who have been called according to His purpose" (Romans 8:28 NIV).

While lying in Christ's arms, I felt safe and filled with love despite all the miserable things I was seeing. I wasn't meant to tell you that I had this wonderful feeling in order to make you think I was somehow privileged, but to help you understand that you can also feel this love and security despite what may happen in the days to come. God's plan is in operation, and all this world's struggles will be resolved for good. While He is driving out the enemy and the battles rage, He safely holds those who love Him in His arms. Just hang on, and let Him carry you.

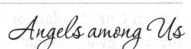

Chapter 6

Angels among Us

"As we moved across the earth, He showed me people working in their daily lives. The only one I clearly remember was a woman who appeared to be a fortune-teller. Jesus proclaimed in a jolly manner, 'Here's My bad one and My good one.' He introduced me to the lady fortune-teller who was holding a card. She told me she was the bad one. On the card there was a little laughing lady who appeared to be having the greatest fun. Jesus introduced her to me as an angel. Jesus told her to tell me what her assignment was. She laughingly told me that her assignment was the fortune-teller. She also jokingly stated that she was 'like an indentured servant,' laughing as if her statement were something of a joke, and Jesus laughed

*with her. He then asked her to share some
of her previous assignments with me. She
held up a long, narrow sheet of paper with
many names listed down its length. Jesus
continued joking and laughing with the
angel as we moved away."*

Jesus didn't say the fortune-teller was not His child.
He said, *"My* bad one." All of us who have followed
a wrong path and broken His commandments are still
His children. I repeatedly turned my back on what He
wanted for me, but He was always ready to counsel me
when I turned to Him. He had to do this repeatedly
until I understood I could not manage without Him.
He can bring us back into the fold and give us a mind
to recognize temptations and deceptions for what they
are. Our fortune-teller needs to recognize who Christ
is and surrender herself to Him. She must recognize
that Christ must come first and that none of us can
survive this life under the false guidance of mysticism,
mediums, fortune-tellers, or other false gods and
spirits.

I don't know whether the angel's assignment was the
misguided fortune-teller, the protection of the fortune-
teller's clientele, or both. I think the importance of this
visit was to understand that Christ considers all of us
His children. It is good to know that there are angels
working among us, even among those practicing evil,

as extensions of God's hands in bringing us through life and to Him. God's Spirit is in action amid sinners just as Jesus was during His earthly ministry.

The obvious joy of this little angel tells me that working for God's kingdom is an exercise in love, and love produces joy. It tells me that a way to recognize people who are filled with the Spirit is to see whether they are joyful. Jesus clearly trusted the angel with her assignment. He seemed like the boss who visits a trusted employee's workstation and jokes with her rather than micromanaging her efforts. This employee trusts her employer enough to use sarcasm. Jesus is proud of her accomplishments as He tells her to show me the list of her past assignments, in which she takes great joy. I must remember the joy of this angel when completing my own assignments. "Serve the Lord with gladness" (Psalm 100:2 NIV). There is nothing holy about going about our service with a serious, piously stern, or judgmental attitude. Nothing repels potential converts to Christianity like a bunch of stiff, rigid congregants who focus on the negatives. Jesus jokes, laughs, and has fun, so we can do the same!

"Are not all angels ministering spirits sent to serve those who will inherit the salvation?" (Hebrews 1:14 NIV). Isn't it comforting to know that even in the presence of wrongdoing, a ministering spirit may be there to protect and serve us? We may be tempted into doing something we know is against God's desires for us, such as seeking the guidance of a fortune-teller rather than turning to Him in prayer. He still works through His servants to disrupt the intentions of the evil one and help us back onto the narrow road. Those servants are humans as well as angels. We do not have to engage in evil in the presence of evil to be available to help pull someone who has been betrayed by evil and has been filled with hopelessness out of the mire. Keep an eye on those who are straying. Let them know you care for them, and be available when they are ready to come back to Christ. Being available means being in the community outside the church walls and being around folks we may not be comfortable with. Our joyful presence and example can make the difference between someone's choice for good and evil.

When I was introduced to the angel, I felt as though I was a new hire meeting a longtime employee. The angels are workers and servants in God's kingdom as are we who accept Christ and the assignments He gives us. We are partners in serving Him. Both the angels and we humans look to our Lord for guidance and supervision. Christ may assign angels to protect us or act as messengers, but we need to regard them as fellow servants of God and not beings to whom we should pray or seek intercession. When people call upon spirits or beings other than God, they are trying to be the bosses. When an employee tries to act like the boss and take over the job of the boss, he or she may end up fired from the company. Remember—Jesus was the boss, and the angel received her assignments from Him. If you think you need the help of an angel, tell God, and trust that He will respond to your need in keeping with His wisdom. He may use an angel to help you, or He may not.

Chapter 7

The Ascent to Heaven

"We then started rising, and as we
ascended I became aware of what seemed
like a sphere over my head with three oval
(on the horizontal) windows—one directly
in front, one to my left, and another to
my right. When I attempted to look out
the front window, a small hand appeared
outside the window to block my view. The
same then happened for the left and right
windows. We stopped rising at a place
Jesus told me contained both joy and
sadness."

I think Christ was protecting me from things I
should not see. A loving father protects his children
from things they are not ready to comprehend. Jesus
could have placed me in darkness but He wanted me
to be aware that there was something out there and

that we were rising. He wanted me to understand that we were moving to another place and that there were things that I should not know, at least not yet. Paul wrote, "I know a man in Christ who fourteen years ago was caught up to the third heaven. Whether it was in the body or out of the body, I do not know. And I know that this man—whether in the body or apart from the body was caught up to paradise. He heard inexpressible things that that man is not permitted to tell" (2 Corinthians 12:2–3 NIV).

I think back to another time the Lord told me that there were things I was not ready to know. In 1976, my father died at the age of forty-nine. We now think he died from a mesothelioma, related to his service in the US Navy during WWII. Mesothelioma, the asbestos-related lung disease, was not recognized as another form of cancer until years later. I was only twenty-five years old. My marriage to my second husband was a year old, and I felt very lonely in my separate bedroom, with the exception of Tiny, the St. Bernard, lying next to the bed. I was praying during another sleepless night. Those prayers were tear-filled requests. I wanted answers about why Dad had died so young. Where had he gone? Would I see him again? A clear, small voice instructed me to get out of bed and face the bedroom door. I did so, and an oval window appeared in the solid wood. A bright light shone through the glass, which appeared frosted and beautifully etched, somewhat like a window frosted with ice crystals. The voice then stated, "Now you see through a glass, darkly." I stood there until the window faded away, and then I immediately went to the nightstand, turned on the light, picked up the Bible lying there, searched the concordance, and found 1 Corinthians 13:12 (KJV), which says, "For now we see through a glass, darkly; but then face to face; now I know in part; but then shall I know even as also I am known."

Although I still terribly missed my father, I lost the feeling of desperation, knowing that God was aware of my grief. Wherever Dad was, God was involved with both his life and mine, and I knew that I would someday have all my questions answered. Just the knowledge that God knew I had questions was comforting.

Those questions were partially answered a few months later when my mother gave me a letter my father had written before he died. He wrote that while he was in the navy, he had contracted scarlet fever and almost died. During this illness he had a vision in which he described two men in glowing white robes discussing whether to admit him to heaven or not. They decided to send him back for a while because his mother would need him in the future. Dad subsequently lived his life with the knowledge that he would not live a full life span. His father had suffered difficulties with gambling that affected my grandmother's well-being, and Dad actively and lovingly engaged with Grandpa in a way that mitigated the devastation that could have occurred. Dad died not long after Grandpa's death. It comforted me to know Dad had his vision because it told me that his life had been in God's hands and that he was now assuredly in heaven.

Chapter 8

People under the Law
and Judgment

"*I saw a line of confused-looking people*
in blue clothing walking in a line under
guard. The guards were large imposing
men, but they were not carrying weapons
that I could see. The people who filed past
me appeared to be East Asian, with one
woman wearing the traditional straw hat
seen on field workers. No one told me, but
I had the impression that this was not a
permanent place for anyone there, that
this was a place for learning. Here there
was also a flurry of confusing rapid activity
with many people milling around."

I think I was in the intermediate realm referred
to in the New Testament as "paradise." I base my

viewpoint on the meaning of the word *paradise* as used by Christ in addressing the thief on the cross. This definition appears in *Baker's Evangelical Dictionary of Biblical Theology* and *Harper's Bible Dictionary*. This viewpoint embraces the concept that *paradise*, as referred to by Paul in 2 Corinthians 12:2–3 (NIV), is a state where the souls of believers wait with our Lord for the final judgment and entry into the new heaven. This is what we call heaven, and we understand that this will change on judgment day. This was the interpretation of the word used by Jews at the time of Christ, and since Christ was a Jewish rabbi, I think He would have expected people to interpret the vernacular of the time using the associated meanings of the time. The most important thing, however, is that wherever believers may be after death, Jesus is there. Whether you agree with this viewpoint or not, I am sure we as Christians can all agree that in the end there will be one heaven and one earth where Christ is King and that the issue of a definition of paradise will be moot. "But in keeping with His promise we are looking forward to a new heaven and a new earth where righteousness dwells" (2 Peter 3:13 NIV).

While I was watching the people in blue, it was apparent that I was in only one part of the place where Jesus had taken me. I was standing to the side of their column as they passed by. They looked straight ahead and never glanced my way. They filed through a doorway into another area. As I proceeded through this journey, which was something like an educational tour, it was evident that there were different rooms or sections.

Because of the confused looks on their faces, I wondered if the people in blue might have been those who had never heard of Christ but knew in their hearts that they had a loving creator and honored Him in their hearts. They looked like they had no idea where they were. I likened the people in blue to herded sheep being filed into a corral. If they knew nothing of Christ or heaven, they would certainly be confused. We could not leave them on their own recognizance anymore than we could leave a kindergartener to wander the halls of school on the first day. Regardless of who they were or why they were there, I think our Lord would find a way to make provision and opportunity for all of us to learn who He is. I know He wants us to be able to choose Him, and if we have no knowledge of Him, we cannot make a choice. This was my impression based upon the feelings I experienced while standing beside the people filing past me that night and what I know about the character of the Lord, who carried me in His arms.

During a discussion of this journey to paradise with a minister friend, it was obvious that he did not share some of my interpretative viewpoints, and he warned me not to place interpretations on the vision that were not biblical. This concerned me, so I prayed regarding the people in blue and remembered what Jesus said to me after ascending with Him, namely that this was not a completely joyful place. Upon further thought and study, Matthew 13:49–50 (NKJV) started to invade my thoughts and gnaw at me. "So it will be at the end of the ages, the angels will come forth, separate the wicked from the just, and cast them into the furnace of fire. There will be weeping and gnashing of teeth." Were the guards angels, and if so, then what? I do not think it is for us to know, at least not yet. After I felt the love Jesus had for me while I was in His arms, I can imagine the indescribable grief He must feel to lose those who do not know or accept Him.

So who is saved? If one were to ask whether the people in blue were saved or not, many Christians would find the answer quite simple. They were saved if they had been baptized. My initial nursing education was done at a hospital school run by the sisters of Saint Francis. We were taught that if we doubted a dying patient had been baptized and there were no time to summon a priest, we should immediately perform the sacrament of baptism ourselves, even if the only water available were our spittle, in order to ensure that the soul of the patient was saved from eternal damnation.

In more recent years, I took a class on the Spirit, one taught by the former dean of a Bible college. Despite receiving many valuable insights, his teaching about baptism disturbed me. He was adamant that salvation for any person able to make the decision is dependent upon baptism by immersion. He based his position on John 3:5 (KJV), which says, "Verily, verily, I say unto thee, Except a man be born of the water and of the spirit, he cannot enter the kingdom of God." Our teacher's interpretation even ruled out those baptized by sprinkling and infant baptism because *new birth* is connected to the symbolic dying with Christ, which is going under the water and then being raised above the surface to a new life. I could not help but think of my childhood friend Cheryl.

Cheryl lived across the street from our family during the years we were in grade school and junior high. She had been born with tetralogy of Fallot, which we called "a hole in her heart" or "blue baby." In those days open-heart surgery was a fantasy. She wasn't expected to live long after birth, but she defied the odds and lived to the age of fourteen. She was a member of the Lutheran church, and as such, she was baptized as an infant by sprinkling. She was a child prodigy at the organ and piano, and she was the accompanist for our high school chorus. Handicap accessibility wasn't yet in the vernacular, so other kids would carry her books at school. She was given extra time to change classes. Either a boy would carry her up the stairs to her next class, or she would count to ten between each step. When we kids played ball in the neighborhood vacant lot, she got a slow walk to first base if the pitcher hit her bat with the ball. She was tiny for her age, and her arms and legs were the diameter of a toddler's. We spent many hours sitting and playing with our dolls or singing together on the porch swing. Cheryl never complained about her situation and had an unnatural maturity, patience with others, and unwavering faith in her Lord. One evening as she was in the kitchen with her mother, ironing a blouse to wear to Luther League, Cheryl collapsed beside the ironing board. Her mother then saw her rise up on her knees, look upward, and exclaim, "My Jesus!" Then she fell again to the floor. Cheryl was gone from us.

When the Bible scholar told our class that only those baptized by immersion were saved, I could not accept it based upon what had happened at Cheryl's death. It upset me so much. I turned to prayer for an answer, and one was given! I received a vivid image in the middle of the night, one of writing that filled my whole field of vision. The calligraphy was undecipherable, similar in appearance to pictures I had seen of ancient scrolls, and I knew it was supposed to be read from right to left. I don't know why I knew this. In the center of the writing was a large purple seal imprinted with the name God.

I interpreted the writing and the seal to be symbolic of the Book of Life. This meant that my question about whether or not Cheryl was with Christ was

God's decision. The book is sealed, and whether her name was written in the Book of Life was up to Him. In Exodus 32:32 (NKJV), upon Moses' plea that his people be forgiven of their sins, the Lord said, "I will erase from my book the names of people who sin against me." The book was then sealed—no ifs, ands, or buts about it. We have all sinned against God, but Christ has covered those sins. The book was sealed so that no other names would be erased. No one knows other than God what is written there. My personal knowledge that Cheryl is with the Lord is expressed so succinctly in John 6:40 (NKJV), which says, "And this is the will of Him who sent me, that all who see the Son and believes in Him may have everlasting life, and I will raise him up at the last day."

Today's practice of Christian baptism is rooted in the Jewish ritual of cleansing in Jesus' day. In the Jewish faith of today (as well as in Jesus' time), immersion is required as part of the requirement for conversion to Judaism to symbolize a cleansing or change of soul (Lamm 2003). There are also several other customary times when immersion is performed, such as Yom Kippur, before marriage, or after childbirth and menstruation. This is done as a sign of repentance or purity. New converts to Judaism in ancient times (as well as today) were usually immersed three times in front of witnesses. The baptismal water, called *Mikveh*, was referred to as "the womb of the world," and coming out of the water was considered a *new birth*. A convert was referred to as "a little child just born," "a new birth" setting the person apart from his or her former pagan life (Moseley, undated). John the Baptist declared,

> I indeed baptize you with water unto repentance, but he who is coming after me is mightier that I whose sandals I am not worthy to carry. He will baptize you with the Holy Spirit and Fire. His winnowing fan is in His hand, and He will thoroughly clean out His threshing floor, and gather His wheat into the barn; but He will burn up the chaff with unquenchable fire. (Matthew 3:11–12 NKJV)

(I liken the word *fire* in verse 11 as symbolic of enlightenment or in reference to the fire that smelts and purifies metal. In verse 12, I interpret "unquenchable fire" as that which goes beyond purification to total annihilation.

There were several different levels of ritual bathing in the ancient Jewish baptismal rite, ranging from the lowest level of a stationary bath to the highest order as a flowing spring or river. This water was called "living water" (Moseley, undated). Jesus refers to Himself as "living water." To the Samaritan woman at Jacob's well,

Christ said, "If you knew the gift of God and who it is that asks you for a drink, you would have asked him and he would have given you living water" (John 4:10 NIV). "Everyone who drinks this (well) water will be thirsty again, but whoever drinks the water I give him will never thirst. Indeed the water I give him will become in him a spring of water welling up to eternal life" (John 4:13 NIV).

Jesus said that He needed to be baptized by John in order to fulfill all righteousness. As a rabbi and a Jew, this was an act of obedience to God that Jesus considered necessary to beginning His ministry. I was baptized as an infant, but I decided in adulthood to be baptized by immersion as an act of obedience, repentance, and purification. It carried great meaning for me and was an important piece of my spiritual healing. Baptism, however, without repentance, does nothing for the soul. I am convinced that repentance and baptism by the spirit without the opportunity for baptism by water does not separate us from eternal life with Christ. "Very truly I tell you, whoever hears my word and believes him who sent me has eternal life and will not be judged, but has crossed over from death to life" (John 5:24 NIV). I also believe that if you have received baptism of the Spirit, you will feel compelled to receive baptism by water as an act of obedience to grow closer in your relationship with our Lord and as an outward expression of what has occurred in your soul.

Symbolism of the Color Blue

Still not feeling satisfied that I fully understood the message embedded in the people in blue, I prayed for further guidance. I was ignoring the obvious, the color blue! The blue worn by these people was the tone and shade of my favorite lapis earrings, but what was its symbolic meaning or significance?

In Exodus 24:9–12 (NKJV), Moses along with Aaron, Nadab, Abihu, and seventy elders of Israel saw God. Paved stone was under God's feet, and it looked like the color of sapphire stone. After this, He took Moses up to Him and gave him tablets carved from stone that contained the written law and the commandments. One could conclude that the stone tablets were also made of this sapphire-like stone, which was likely blue too. In Ezekiel's vision of God, he wrote that the throne that appeared above the firmament (sky), looked like sapphire, and that it had the likeness of a man sitting upon it. The foundation of heaven is sapphire-like stone, and the foundation of the Hebrew religion is the law.

In the laws given to Moses and Aaron by God regarding care of the most holy things in the tabernacle, they were instructed to spread blue cloth on the table where the showbread was placed and to cover the pans, bowls, pitchers, and dishes with blue cloth. They were then instructed to place the utensils in a blue cloth. The golden altar and the lamp stead were also to be covered with a blue cloth (Numbers 4:7, 9, 11–12 NKJV).

The Lord instructed Moses to place tassels on the corners of their garments that were to include a blue thread. "And you shall have the tassel that you may look upon it and remember all the commandments of the Lord and do them" (Numbers 15:38–39 NKJV.) In Exodus 28:31 (NKJV), the Lord instructed that the ephod was to be blue. The ephod was a garment covering front and back, held together with shoulder straps. It was placed over a priest's robe, on top of which was placed the breastplate (Miller and Miller, 1952).

So what am I getting at with this little study? Some believe that the first writing of the commandments and God's law were carved from blue (sapphire-like) stone. God stood on sapphire-like stone to deliver the commandments. The throne from which He rules is made of sapphire-like stone. The garment tassels that are supposed to remind wearers of the commandments were to include a blue thread. The sacred altar and tabernacle objects were covered with a blue cloth. The priests' robes were covered in a blue cloth. Blue is related to God's Word, to the law, and to covering. My interpretation is that the people in blue were covered. They were under the law. They were under judgment. Those of us who know and believe in Christ are no longer under the law, but we are covered by saving grace through Christ's sacrifice on the cross. A relationship with Christ gives us personal access to God through the presence of His Spirit. Christian believers are not separated from God by the cover of the law.

Consider my question in the previous chapter about those who may know in their hearts that there is one true God, the Creator of all things, and who diligently seek a relationship with him but have never been introduced to Christ or Christianity. Hebrews 11:1 (NKJV) states, "Now faith is the substance of things hoped for, and the evidence of things not seen." In Hebrews 11:13–16 (NKJV), Paul describes those who died in faith, having discerned through that faith that there is something more for them beyond this earthly existence. He writes of those who see themselves as strangers or sojourners on this earth and seek another homeland or heaven, where their Creator lives. Verse 16 states, "Therefore God is not ashamed to be called their God, for he has prepared a city for them." Therefore, I think there is a possibility that the Lord considers one or more of the people in blue under judgment for admission to that special city, the one about which Paul wrote. It is also not for us to know to whom God grants eternal life. As rank-and-file employees, would it be our business to decide whom the owner and operations manager of our workplace selects to work with us? God is the owner, and Jesus is the operations manager of heaven.

I am convinced that to trust and believe in one part of the triune God is to believe in all parts—the Father, the Son, and the Holy Spirit. When we experience any part, we as believers will recognize it, even if we have never been taught about its existence. Conversely, to reject any part of the triune God is to reject the whole.

Chapter 9

Heavenly Mentors, Lessons, and Assignments

"A small group of us was then gathered and ushered through a door into a quiet place where we met a seated panel, including some of the people I had seen on my earthly round with Jesus. A leader introduced each. A member of the panel introduced us to a tall, very handsome black man named Mask. While being introduced, Mask's beautiful face morphed into a rustic, brown, flat, African tribal mask with slits for eyes. This man explained that the handsome face was only for his earthly work and that he had chosen to have the cracked, brown, distorted face where we were to remind him of the things he once did and the way he had once been."

The interview occurred in a separate room with the panel members seated in a row in front of us, facing the door. There were four or five members. A light-skinned male seated to the right made the introductions and served as the spokesman at the second meeting with the panel.

Some nonbelievers ascribe to the idea that upon death, we enter into some kind of collective consciousness. Some believe in a greater power or god but say that upon death we are somehow absorbed into his being. Others believe that we are transformed into other beings or reincarnated. Mask's words made it clear to me that we remain *us*, that we are still individuals after our earthly deaths, and that we make decisions. I am sure that God didn't make this man wear the mask as a punishment for past deeds but that he *chose* to wear the mask to represent what God had done for him and the fact that our Lord rescues the lost. Based on the mask's design, this man could have once lived in the darkness of an animist or polytheistic religion. That he spoke of the person he once was indicated to me that he was as not an angel.

One could draw a parallel between Mask and the apostle Matthew. It is interesting to note that in the books of Mark and Luke, Matthew is referred to as Levi, which was the name given to him by Jesus, which means "gift of the Lord." In the book of Matthew, however, he refers to himself as "Matthew the Tax

Collector," obviously as a reminder of the person he was before he was renamed by Jesus (Matthew 9:9–13; Mark 2:14 NKJV). It was Matthew's choice to call himself a "tax collector" after he had abandoned that life.

The fact that I also saw some of the people on the panel in the walk on earth suggests to me that God does not stop using those who are in Him for His purpose after our earthly deaths. If we are in Christ, we will continue working in His kingdom to help bring about a new heaven and a new earth. The place I visited was active and busy. Each person I saw moved with a purpose. It was apparent to me that we do not just float about in some sort of inert, suspended state until judgment day. Regardless of where believers go after death, Jesus is there. He wants us to be His friends and family, and as such, we can work and play beside Him in His kingdom.

> *"I was then rapidly moved, giving me a feeling of being sucked or whooshed to another place. The sensation was almost dizzying. Here I observed many people involved in all types of activities in rapid succession. At times I found myself walking with another person, a female. I found I bounced when I stepped, and I had a bit of trouble controlling my trajectory.*

It was so easy to bounce up stairs. My companion laughingly told me, 'It takes a little getting used to.' As we spent time in that area, things were conveyed to me, little by little, like a mental puzzle. I was told, 'Be moderate,' more than once. I was also told a Bible verse about sharing what had been revealed to me and again to be moderate."

Bouncing up the stairs was a fun interlude. I learned, however, that wherever I was, it was an actual place and that I had senses. Was this a sample of how it would feel to be in the new body I would someday inherit? I felt like a little child who just had fun moving and discovering what her body could do. I like to imagine how I'll be able to twirl about and dance! I want to run, play, and jump into the air when I get back there! There were no cares, just joy in the moment. I was like a little child. Thinking back, I cannot help but wonder if the young woman who joined me on the stairs was Cheryl from my childhood. It would be appropriate that I would now see her bounding up the stairs, laughing and happy. I would not have easily recognized her in a healthy body.

When I was in my twenties, I was diagnosed with rheumatoid arthritis. My joints would swell, and the pain was excruciating. During the ensuing years, it has become apparent that the diagnosis was probably wrong. The joint swelling disappeared after a few years of high-dose aspirin and hydroxychloroquine therapy (referred to as synthetic quinine), but the pain and stiffness remained. Whatever the disorder may be, recent years have renamed the pain as fibromyalgia. In 2003, I experienced a back injury that eventually resulted in multilevel spinal fusion. The surgery was not effective in relieving my lower back and leg pain. This nerve pain, combined with the fibromyalgia, has made freedom of movement a challenge at times. I tire easily and must plan my weekly activities to allow for periods of recuperation. I cannot tolerate opiate pain medication because it induces severe nausea, not to mention the mind-numbing side effects of common drugs for the treatment of fibromyalgia. If I spend several hours volunteering for a local charity, I must set aside that evening for rest. If I go out with friends for an evening of dinner and playing cards, I must set aside the following morning for rest. If I do grocery shopping in the morning, I must find quiet activity or take a nap in the afternoon. Every day is a challenge to maintain strength, flexibility, and endurance. The freedom from pain and unlimited ability to move while in paradise was exquisite. The fact that all of our infirmities will disappear is true! What better thing is there to look forward to other than the ability to run about freely without tiring, to have even greater energy than my four-year-old whirlwind of a grandson? How much easier it will be to live and serve in God's kingdom when unhampered by pain and fatigue!

> *"I and the other members of my group who previously met with the panel were once again before them. We were asked one by one if we figured out our assignments. I was so caught up in discerning what my own answer was to be that I didn't pay close attention to the others' answers. I remember the individual beside me saying something to the effect that he was to bring happiness to other people. I was thrilled and anxious to share what I had learned and still filled with the feeling of bliss from having been held in Christ's arms. My answer was that I was to share this experience with the world. The panel then reiterated, 'Be moderate.'"*

It is interesting that instead of just being told our purpose in being there, our group was given experiences and gradually fed information to process so that we came to conclusions based upon our own deductions. Was this a test to see if our thinking was in line with the Savior's? Was this whole experience a sort of preemployment test, one that was necessary before ever discussing job assignments? We are told in 2 Peter 1:10 (NIV) to make an effort to confirm our callings instead of being handed a calling. God expects an effort in critical thinking from this experience. I believe Christ wants us to develop our thinking and understanding so that we not only work for Him with effective purpose but also can carry on a real relationship with Him that consists of two-way communication and continually builds a loving bond. As He reveals the truth to us and as we are able to accept and understand the truth, we become like-minded with Him. As such, He can increasingly trust us with the work of His kingdom. "Therefore, my brothers and sisters, make every effort to confirm your calling and election. For if you do these things, you will never stumble" (2 Peter 1:10 NIV).

Preparations for a Great Feast

Understanding what the admonition to "be moderate" meant came weeks after the vision. It is obvious that the Lord doesn't want me to make emotionally charged proclamations that incite religious fervor. I believe Christ wants me to share this experience in order to help people come to a fuller relationship with Him. Doing so is certainly an emotional experience but one of contemplation, study, listening, and prayer.

Evangelism isn't a matter of creating a sort of religious hysteria but of bringing light into what was darkness through a ministry of physical, spiritual, and emotional healing. I fall far short of His glory. I am a work in progress, and I have been asked to deliver a message. I am only a conduit, and I had no part in creating the message.

Several weeks after pondering the meaning of the "be moderate" directive, I went to bed with the repetitive prayer. I was becoming frustrated with trying to figure out what I was supposed to be moderate about because the basic understandings I'd derived from the *journey* were nothing that couldn't be figuratively shouted from the mountaintops. In other words, I nagged, "Please give me a hint!" I was startled awake at around five in the morning. I sat up in bed, and that now familiar voice said, "Remember the feast."

I had the vivid vision about a feast in 1998. I had attended an educators' conference near Salt Lake City, Utah. One of my fellow participants who took a few of us on a tour of the area shared that her son had converted to the Mormon religion and was marrying a girl who was a member. She told us that she was disheartened because she and her husband couldn't see the wedding ceremony, let alone participate in it, because they were Lutheran and not worthy to enter the temple where their son was saying his vows. I thought this was so unfortunate for her, considering that none of us is worthy to enter God's temple without the sacrifice made by Christ. We *unworthy* people are so blessed that Jesus paid the debt for our sins in full so that we may enter heaven, even if we cannot enter the man-made temple.

Several days later I had this woman and the Mormon temple in mind as I drifted off to sleep. I found myself strolling down a large boulevard that had no one in the street or on the sidewalk. I looked up at a large, imposing temple across the street on my right, and I sarcastically thought, *Humph, wonder if I'm worthy to enter that building.* I then realized a young woman was walking beside me on my left. She said, "Let me show you something. Come with me." I followed her across the street, to the right of the temple, and down some stairs to a side door. She opened the door, and we both entered, standing just inside.

There before us was a great long table set with platters of food, running the length of the wall to our right. Women were carrying additional magnificent platters of colorful, delicious-looking food. There was a flurry of quiet, purposeful activity all over the room. In the background I could hear a choir singing the most beautiful music I had ever heard. I had the impression that the singers were practicing. A great celebration was being prepared. I want to sing with that choir!

We now celebrate a communion feast with fellow Christians in remembrance of Jesus as He instructed at

His Last Supper (the Jewish Passover) with his apostles. Our Communion of bread and wine also reminds us that we are passed over by eternal death because Christ has covered our symbolic doors with His blood. He is our Passover Lamb. When we join Jesus in heaven, our Communion meal with Him will be the most magnificent feast we could ever imagine. I don't just think of His sacrifice when I take Communion, but I also anticipate the great party to come.

In conjunction with my great journey with Jesus, this experience tells me that preparations are being made for a great heavenly event, that God's people are being asked and mobilized like never before to share God's good news of salvation, and that now is the time to come home to God's family if you have not done so. The next part of my journey suggests to me that the gates of New Jerusalem are opening.

Chapter 10

Choose Your Gate to Heaven or Hell

"After learning our assignments, we found ourselves walking along a great corridor in the midst of a multitude of other people. We walked up to a series of two vertically rectangular portals, through which I could only see light. As I approached the first set of portals, I heard a man somewhere behind me in the crowd state that it was important to select the correct door. Not able to discern a difference between the two portals and feeling anxiety about this, I closed my eyes and allowed myself to remember the blissful sensation of being in Christ's arms and found myself whooshed through a portal. Continuing on to the next set of portals or gates, I suddenly *found that a man was trying to pull me into a portal by my right hand. A good-looking but malevolent being was pulling the man's right hand, while the man's left hand pulled mine. I yanked my hand out of his and stepped back to watch. Jesus was standing to my right, and the man was to my left. The man was looking at Jesus with a questioning expression. Jesus said to him, "It's your choice," and the man allowed himself to be pulled into the portal by the malevolent being. I again closed my eyes, remembering being held in Christ's arms, and was whooshed through the next portal ... and then another."*

This is the most impactful and momentous part of my journey. The doorways, portals, gates (I am not sure what to call them) had bright white light shining through them, so I could not see what was on the other side. They appeared in pairs. One looked identical to the other, so it was impossible for me to discern the correct one based upon my own knowledge and perception. Placing myself totally in Jesus' control, not even using my own eyes or standing on my own feet, was the only way I could pass through. I think this represents that we cannot get to heaven and cannot pass through the gates of New Jerusalem without complete surrender to Christ. *"I am the way and the truth and the life. No one comes to the father except through me"* (Luke 13:23–24 NIV).

The man, who was holding on to me and then allowed himself to be pulled into the wrong portal was a somewhat paunchy, middle-aged, dark-haired fellow dressed in business attire. He knew who Jesus was. I think he possibly thought that by holding on to me, I could pull him through the correct portal, that by attaching himself to a believer, he could find the door to eternal life. His nonverbal exchange with Christ seemed to indicate that he wanted someone to tell him what to do in order to enter the kingdom of heaven. Jesus made it clear that choosing Him was a matter of this man's free choice. It was a choice, however, to fully trust and turn himself over to Christ. It is not enough to know that Jesus is the Son of God. There is only one thing we can *do* to enter the right portal into eternal life. We must give ourselves to Him and totally *believe in* Him. Believing means surrendering our will, trusting and depending upon Him. I think this is what Christ refers to as "the narrow door." No amount of prayer, fasting, tithing, worshipping, or giving to the poor will get us into heaven without surrendering ourselves into His arms. "Someone asked him, 'Lord, are only a few people going to be saved?' He said to them, 'Make every effort to enter through the narrow door because many I tell you, will try to enter and will not be able to'" (Luke 13:23–24 NIV).

"While on this transit through the portals, I recognized that a person who was part of our group and also had an assignment, was someone I was acquainted with on earth, someone I knew but never had a desire to get to know. I attempted to make contact with her during our transit but was unsuccessful. I didn't see her again. Upon return to the earth, but still in the unseen dimension, I ran into people I had met as workers in the other realm, one being a beautician."

None of these people acknowledged me, nor I them. I think this is significant, because we do not always know who truly believes in Christ. Many of us have assignments that, if we carry them out, will increase God's glory and expand His kingdom. We do not always know whose actions represent the work of a heavenly assignment. Those with whom we avoid socialization, have no friends in common, or deem objectionable to our sense of propriety may be working for the kingdom of heaven. Therefore, we should be careful not to judge another's service based upon our own understanding.

Needless to say, we all don't take trips to heaven to receive our assignments. We receive them through the still, small voice and other signs. We prepare to hear what He says to us by quieting ourselves through prayer, a Christ-centered study of scripture, and an open heart. God speaks at His time. Do not expect to hear His voice when you ask Him to speak to you. Do not expect to receive His personal message in a way you expect. You cannot will God to reveal Himself to you, but you must simply be ready to receive Him. The key is to listen and to follow. The Word is not just the Bible, but it includes His personal words to you, that will always be biblically supported. "Do not merely listen to the word, and so deceive yourselves. Do what it says" (James 1:22 NIV). Doing "what it says" requires an understanding of the Word and a "mind of Christ," from the perspective of Christ, rather than from our own frames of reference.

We may hear His calls, and they may tug at our hearts; however, we may fail to recognize them for what they are, or we may choose to ignore them. It is not enough to be fans of Jesus, but we must believe in Him to the extent that we subjugate our will to His will. This is not hard to do or unpleasant because Jesus is love itself. It is a matter of letting ourselves go, placing ourselves in His arms, and trusting Him like a little child trusts a loving father. "Take my yoke upon you and learn from Me, for I am gentle and lively in heart, and you will find rest for your souls; For My yoke is easy and my burden is light" (Matthew 11:29–30 NKJV).

When challenged or persecuted about this choice, remember the eternal home He is preparing for us. Sharing these visions and the scriptures to which they lead me place me directly in the line of fire. I ask you to pray for me so that I will endure whatever nonbelievers, skeptics, and even Satan may throw at me. "And you will be hated by all for my name's sake, but he who endures to the end will be saved" (Matthew 10:22 NKJV). I also pray that you will share the truths you may have learned through my witness.

Chapter 11

A Synopsis of Messages

1. Jesus sees us as His children to love and to teach. He wants us to relate to Him as trusting children who take what He says to heart. He wants to hold and comfort us. Let him. He is big enough to know all of us and carry us when we need Him to.

2. The woes of this world are truly horrible and getting worse. Within the context of our short existence here, we can become disillusioned and fearful. God will ultimately make everything right. He is in charge.

3. Angels exist and work among us in the most unexpected places and among both the righteous and unrighteous. Being in the service of the Lord is a joy-filled occupation. Christ enjoys not only our company but the company of the angels as well.

4. Although we often think of His sacrifice and the tortured image on the cross, He is now

victorious. That means He is a towering, strong, powerful, joyful and happy Lord who can laugh and appreciate a joke. Therefore, when we pray, let us not just bring Him our concerns and needs but tell Him about our joys as well. Share a good joke with Him. Ask Him to dance with you in your new shoes. Tell him you love Him.

5. The unseen dimension of the angels here on earth exists as well as the dimension of the present heaven. Heaven is a place. There are things about moving between these dimensions that we are not yet supposed to see or know, if ever. Jesus is our only connection to the heavenly dimension.

6. Those people who do not know Christ are under judgment by the laws God gave Moses. Only God knows who is saved. There is a place for those who love God but had no introduction to Christ in their earthly lives (e.g., Jews of the pre-Christian era). This is all up to God. It is none of our business. "For my thoughts are not your thoughts, neither are your ways my ways" (Isaiah 55:8 NIV).

7. Those who know who Christ is and do not accept Him choose Satan by default. We can be sure of eternal life if we believe in Jesus Christ. "For God so loved the world that he gave his only son, that whoever believes in him shall not perish but have eternal life" (John 3:16 NIV).

8. There are no religious practices or rituals we can perform to help us enter eternal heaven. We cannot earn our way into heaven by being *good*. We become *good* through a relationship with Christ. The requirement for eternal life is belief in Christ. There is a difference between knowledge and belief. Satan knows every verse of the Bible, and He also knows that Jesus is the Son of God. Belief means placing our full trust in Him, and surrendering our understanding for His wisdom. It means to place ourselves under His control.

9. We are separate and unique individuals in heaven as well as on earth. We are free to make choices and decisions in heaven and on earth. After our earthly deaths, we continue to learn and grow as individual persons in relationship with Christ.

10. Relationship with Christ also means relationship with our brothers and sisters who are believers in Him. We are part of a *whole*, which forms what Christians call "the body of Christ" on earth as well as in heaven. It is a family. Our assignments involve the building and strengthening of the body of Christ here on earth. We increase our understanding of His Word through study and interaction with fellow family members and within the context of our personal relationships with Jesus.

11. There are different *rooms* or places in heaven for different purposes.

12. There is no pain, fatigue, or disability in heaven.

13. Christ is a teacher in the Socratic method. (Or God taught this method!) He presents scenarios and asks questions that lead from one level of understanding to another. Christ uses His workers to facilitate the teaching of lessons that require critical thinking on our part, and then He builds on that learning. He does not dictate our responses to His lessons. He gives us the support and tools to do His work, but it is up to us to do discern what our jobs are to be and to follow through.

14. Jesus is preparing an eternal place for His believers, a new heaven, and a new earth. His people and angels are participating in these preparations. There will be a great celebration when everyone is ready for moving day at Christ's great coming-back party. The preparations are almost complete.

To the Churches

Christians are one body and one church. Belief in Christ is the only ticket to heaven, so the desire to develop a relationship with Him should be the only ticket to church membership and participation in the Lord's Supper. We should be baptized when we have accepted Christ as our Savior. That is an outward expression of the new lives we have already received through baptism of the Spirit. This symbolizes—but does not cause—entry into a new life as part of the Christian family. The method of a baptism doesn't determine whether one will enter the kingdom of heaven. Apart from bringing non-Christians to faith as well as teaching and nourishing the Body of Christ, the churches must not only attest that there is just one body of Christ, but they must act on that basis. In order to strengthen God's kingdom here in our earthly dimension, churches must strive to discard the beliefs and practices that separate Christians. As individuals, we can start by embracing all fellow believers, not just those in our own congregation or denomination, as members of the same family. Differences start pulling us apart when we lean on our own understanding of seemingly ambiguous or conflicting biblical passages and create interpretations that we then embrace as tenets of our faith. Accept that there may be different viewpoints within the same family, but do not allow them to create family rifts. Satan uses the time-tested approach of dividing and conquering. There are no religious denominations in heaven. There will be no religious denominations on the new earth or in the new heaven.

References

Elwell, Walter A. *Baker's Evangelical Dictionary of Biblical Theology*. Grand Rapids, MI: Baker Books, 1996.

Lamm, Rabbi Maurice. My Jewish Learning. "Why Immerse in the Mikveh?" Accessed August 1, 2015. http://www.myjewishlearning.com/article/why-immerse-in-the-mikveh.

Miller, Madeline, and J. Lane Miller. *Harper's Bible Dictionary*, 6th ed. New York: Harper & Brothers, 1952.

Moseley, Ron (PhD). Arkansas Institute of Holy Land Studies. "The Jewish Background of Christian Baptism." Accessed August 5, 2015. http://www.haydid.org/ronimmer.htm.

About the Author

M ary Keenan, nicknamed Sis, was born in Lancaster County, Pennsylvania, where she began a career in nursing and nursing administration. She is founder of one of the first hospice programs in the United States. Mary was a Pennsylvania-licensed nursing home administrator, a health care consultant, a psychiatric nurse manager, a regional nursing director for corporate long-term care companies, and a health care cost-containment manager for a Fortune 500 corporation. Mary taught for West Virginia University Institute of Technology as an associate professor of vocational education. She holds a baccalaureate degree in nursing and master's degrees in education leadership, as well as adult and technical education.

She and her husband, Dale, live in West Virginia, along with their dog, Casey, and two cats, Barney and Thumper. Now retired, Mary has pursued her love of art for the past several years—that is, until the experience of July 2015, when she found herself compelled to become an author of this book. Her art has appeared and won awards in several regional and national art shows, and people can view her work online at www.hiddenwoodsfineart.com. She also enjoys volunteering at her local Salvation Army and crocheting prayer shawls in her spare time.

Mary is a member of the First Christian Church, Disciples of Christ, in Weirton, West Virginia, where she has found a family that mirrors many of the ideals for the body of Christ described in this manuscript.

Printed in the United States
by Bookmasters

Printed in the United States
By Bookmasters